UNRAVELED

And Made Whole Again

Jeremiah 29:11

Destiny,
I pray my story blesses you.
As I mentioned I grew up listening
to your family sing. Keep working
for Jesus ♡
　　Love in Christ,
　　　　Deanna Wood Priddy
　　　2023

Trilogy Christian Publishers

A Wholly Owned Subsidary of Trinity Broadcasting Network

2442 Michelle Drive

Tustin, CA 92780

For information, address Trilogy Christian Publishing

Rights Department, 2442 Michelle Drive, Tustin, Ca 92780.

For information about special discounts for bulk purchases, please contact Trilogy Christian Publishing.

Manufactured in the United States of America

10 9 8 7 6 5 4 3 2 1

Library of Congress Cataloging-in-Publication Data is available.

ISBN 978-1-64773-750-4

ISBN 978-1-64773-751-1 (ebook)

CHAPTER 1

As I sit in my dining room just off the kitchen, I hear drums thumping from the front room. That would be my husband, who is a drummer. Not just any drummer, the best drummer. In my book, anyway.

The sun has just gone down and I am sipping coffee as I try to lay down words to tell you about my past fifty three wonderful, and very adventurous, years on this earth. Wonderful years I say, yes, because God has been good to me in so many ways. I am blessed with two sweet daughters who are A and B Honor students and at the time of this writing, are attending Southern Methodist University. My oldest is starting her third year in college and my youngest her second year. As this writing takes time, I will update you on any changes in my life at the end of this book.

Things were not always this smooth. You see I grew up as a preacher's daughter. I wasn't just a typical preacher's daughter I truly felt the call of God for ministry of my own someday. I loved the revivals, most of all I loved God. I guess you could say my father was fiery preacher. He had silver in his black hair and sweet dark brown eyes with warm hands that would make any cold heart melt. He wasn't always a preacher. My dad was a preacher's kid too. Yep, that honorary preacher's son that stole my mother's heart at the age of fourteen years. They married in Gainesville, Texas, Dad was fifteen and mom was fourteen years old. I think he could have stolen any girl's heart, but my mother was the lucky one. Lucky in so many ways or blessed really. They made it forty-three years through the ups and downs of life with many adventures most people can only dream of.

After working in Las Vegas, where I and my older sister of five years were born, mom and dad moved back home. On the trip back to their home in Oklahoma I guess I gave my sisters and my mom a very tiring trip. I was only a baby and I cried all the way to

Oklahoma from Las Vegas I am told. Dad said that is why I have such a strong singing voice.

When they arrived back in Ardmore, Oklahoma, Dad started his painting and drywall business and mom busied herself with keeping our home and raising us girls; four of us to be exact.

I was in kindergarten and I loved it when my dad came home for lunch and Paul Harvey filled the air with "the rest of the story." I remember so well the sun shining through the front screen door with a spring breeze blowing through. Dad in his white painter pants and mom pouring sweet tea and serving sandwiches.

Sleeping in on Sunday was a usual thing in our house but this Sunday morning when I woke up my mom was ironing a shirt and dad was drinking coffee. My sisters were running around looking for hair pins and hair spray. I was not fully aware of what was happening. All I knew was my oldest sister Sheila had been to a Pentecostal revival and she had given her heart to God and my dad had a dream he missed the rapture. Not to mention they had to bring another sister Theresa home from church like a drunk person. They said she was high on the Holy Ghost. Whatever that was, I wasn't sure, I wanted to see that Ghost if it made her act like that.

That morning, we wound up at a little Assembly of God church just a few blocks from our house. I had been taken to a room they called "Sunday School". I joined in with other kids as we played a fishing game, something about being fishers of men. Then we sang a song that told the devil he could go sit on a tack.

I went back into the main auditorium where joyful music was being played by musicians on a stage. I was so amazed that I couldn't help but stare in awe. A man stood up at the pulpit and he spoke with a strong and powerful voice. He began to preach about Jesus and how He came to save us and give us life. My whole family listened as if they had heard directly from God. Apparently, my dad did.

My dad made a lot of changes in his life. He threw out his beer and cigarettes, he started acting sweeter than normal. So much was changing and then he told us he was going to begin preaching. Well, I did not know where that decision would lead us, but I am going to tell you my memory of it all.

CHAPTER 2

I remember walking holding my mom's hand, I felt the grass that was dry from the summer sun stick through my sandals into my feet. I saw a huge tent, a circus sized tent. I heard the most wonderful sounds of music coming from inside. It was as if the whole earth shook from the beats of the drums and the guitars along with an organ and singing like angels. The jubilant singing and lifting of arms in the air, praises lifted to God, I knew it was going to be an exciting night of church.

A man got up and began to talk about a pile of crutches and wheelchairs that lay beside the platform. He spoke of ambulances bringing in sick people to get prayed for. He told how the Lord would heal them and they came back to testify about it. Doctors testified that they could not believe what was taking place. They documented some of these people, so we knew it had to be so.

I personally saw the pile of wheelchairs and crutches. I saw ambulances who had brought people who were sick to be prayed for. They said God can heal you if only you ask Him. That night I saw many get up and walk out praising God for a miracle. Along with all of this going on, the preacher man said he was taking shoes to the poor and if you felt led to give your shows so a needy person could have them then take them off right now. Give them to God! We went home that night without shoes on.

Something happened under that tent that night that stirred my parent's heart. My family would not be the same ever again.

One night, my dad was hurrying home after work just outside of a small town Marietta, Oklahoma. He was pulled over by a local police officer and was asked why he was speeding. My dad told him he was in a hurry because he wanted to get home to get ready to go to church. The police officer gave him a ticket and sent him on his way. Dad headed back on the highway when he saw the police officer again in his rear-view mirror with his lights on. Dad thought *oh no what did I do now?* The officer walked up to his window and said, "Let me see that ticket." Dad handed it to him, and the officer said, "I don't feel right giving this to you." And tore it up.

It wasn't long until we were printing fliers with pictures and words that said *Anointed Preaching and Gospel Singing*! These were passed out in the neighborhood of a church that no one had ever heard of, Miracle Deliverance Temple. This little church sat in the city of Ardmore, Oklahoma on D street. Both of my parents were born in Ardmore, so this was going to be a challenge for my parents to pastor a church in the town they grew up in. Dad proceeded to start this little church with his assistant pastor Charles Ryan. Charles and his family became very dear to my family. They had two sons that played music with my sisters and me. In fact, my sister Belinda taught their son Johnny to play the drums. Steve was taught to play the organ by my sister Theresa. Something interesting is that Johnny taught my husband Kirk to play the drums. I still have the drum set that Belinda used to teach Johnny.

As Theresa, Belinda, and I were gifted in music, my oldest sister Sheila enjoyed art and became a very good artist. To this day, she still paints beautiful pictures. I have always admired her as she is a big part of how my family took the path we did. My next to oldest sister, Theresa, can sing like an angel and she took up playing the organ. Not just any organ it was a B3 Hammond organ! Revival sounds filled the air as she played like no one else could. Belinda, my sister under her and five years my elder, she began learning the drums after watching another preacher's kid play drums in a tent revival. She was, and still is, so good at playing those drums and has a beautiful singing voice.

I remember the sounds of that music that came from the instruments my sisters Theresa and Belinda played. The crowds began to grow as word spread about our church. Soon we had preachers coming from Dallas to hold revivals, one that has been a family friend since, he was a young slim tall man who preached like no one else! He had the power when he spoke! He would start preaching then close his eyes. You knew when he closed his eyes he was getting into the spirit. He was David Gore and I will never forget that Texas drawl in his soft raspy voice. We also had one from a faraway island of cannibals. Yes, cannibals! He was about four feet tall with a wife close to six feet tall it seemed. He spent hours telling us how he used to eat missionaries and would barbecue them for dinner. He had stowed away on a ship after a missionary led him to Christ. As my sister and I lay in our beds we could hear our folks visiting with him and his wife in the living room. He heard us giggle and for some reason thought it was funny to say, "I'm Getting Hungry!" Quickly, we covered our heads and tried not to breathe too loudly. Trusting my dad would protect us if he turned back into a cannibal.

During this time Dad took prayer very seriously. I remember mom made him a sackcloth shirt and he took a cardboard box filled with ashes and he laid in it for what seemed like a week or more. He did this at our church, and he did not eat, and he prayed to God asking for His will and to show us His miracles. He had a vision that God told him, "Here is your guardian angel, he has been assigned to you. His name is Vision and Revelation." Dad said the angel he saw was over nine feet tall and carried a big sword. It wasn't long until we started seeing the miracles that Dad sought God for.

Dad was asked to go pray for a man who was dying of cancer. His family had been called in to his hospital room to make arrangements to say goodbye. Dad walked into the room as I watched from the doorway. Dad said this man does not have to die of this cancer. The family looked at Dad like he was crazy. Dad took the man's hand and said, "Brother, do you believe in Jesus?" He began to pray with this man and he then spoke with boldness to the cancer. He told the cancer to leave his body. My father asked God to restore him and make him whole in the name of Jesus! That man walked out a week or so later and was made whole! No cancer! No death! He lived many more years.

CHAPTER 3

Psalms 91:11

I was in second grade, my sister, Belinda was in seventh grade. Things began to get a bit weird as a call came into our home and someone asked to speak to me. It was a mother of a boy in my class who started accusing me of pushing her son at recess and how she would cut me into pieces next time I came to school. I began to cry, and dad took the phone screaming, "Who is this?!"

It wasn't much time later and Belinda was jumped on by a boy. He attacked her out of nowhere for no reason and she hit him with her purse as he ran away. That was the sign my dad needed to close-up shop and go on the road. But first there is Mexico.

On Christmas morning, my parents loaded us up into the little orange van and we waved goodbye to my grandparents as we headed to Old Mexico.

My father had made the mission trip a couple of times before with two other ministers and my brother in law. They met with our host and interpreter, Pastor Lazarus.

I remember the long journey across Texas and how we crossed the border at night. The smell in the air was somehow different as if we entered another world. I was so excited and scared at the same time. Billboards of Santa with words I wasn't able to read were everywhere and in my child's mind I was amazed that it was Christmas time there too. The long night journey took us into Mexico City. I remember the glow of the amber colored streetlights as the dust arose from the dirt roads.

My dad drove our little orange van into a gas station parking lot. Our interpreter spoke to the gas attendant, as I went with my mother to the ladies' room. Not realizing that my mother had returned to our van, as she thought I was already back in the van. When I tried to open the rusty hinged door, I couldn't open it.

I became a little scared as I heard two men talking and laughing. I guess they knew my situation and thought it was funny. The doorknob shook, and the door came open and I ran straight out to my mother crying. I just knew I had been left in this strange city that I didn't understand.

I remember arriving the first day. We pulled in through a big gate with about ten feet tall white walls of stone attached, and the walls were covered on top with broken glass. We stayed in the tabernacle, which also housed the interpreter and his wife and two children.

As I lay in my little cot trying to sleep, gunshots rang out and there was a horrible scream of a woman out in the street. You see, there was a sugar war going on with soldiers all along the streets. I was afraid that I might get shot as we went to the market.

The banana and goat milk milkshakes were very good! In the market alongside the chocolate covered crickets, were sugar cane and raw meat of all kinds just sitting out in the open and not refrigerated at all. The beautiful dresses and ponchos hung on hooks while festive music filled the air. We bought our bottled water and warm bottled Pepsi and my favorite, Gansitos, a very good dark chocolate cupcake.

The interpreter took us to the ancient ruins of the Aztecs and my imagination ran wild as I walked through the doors and rooms that used to house many ancient peoples of Mexico. It was one of the most beautiful places I have ever seen.

We traveled up into a mountain village called Patchutla. My father was supposed to preach there in a tiny church. I remember the excitement of the people as we arrived. It was a very primitive village with no running water, toilets, electricity, or air conditioning. As my father stood outside with a bowl of water and razor shaving his face in the mirror, several children ran up to him laughing. You see he had shaving cream on his face and they had never seen anything like that. We really made them happy when we gave out the toys our church had sent them.

While my sister Belinda and I hid out in our van, our family, with our interpreter, gathered at the dining table of our gracious hosts. The table was outside, and the ground was swept and watered down to make it smooth and for the dust to settle. Pigs and chickens ran through their feet as the hosts stood behind them watching to see that they ate the food they had prepared for them. It was fish soup and iguana tamales. The iguana tamales were made of the feet from an iguana with toenails intact. My father said the toenails were to be used as toothpicks. Haha! The fish soup was passed around and my sister took her serving and on top was a floating eyeball. It was given to the guest as a special treat. She gently nudged the interpreter and asked him to take it. Thankfully for her, he did. Meanwhile, my sister Belinda and I are in playing in the van, several young men and boys had climbed on top to check out this new thing that had come into their village. It probably drew more attention than normal since my dad liked bright colors and had painted it orange.

The next day headed back down to the tabernacle my dad became very ill. He began to vomit and run a fever. The interpreter felt sure he had been poisoned. We never really knew, but it was a long trip back to the tabernacle. Dad began to feel better and we all were happy that he was. My dad asked what, "Was that awful smell in the van?" When we stopped for gas he told us to look and see if the interpreter's wife had changed a baby's diaper and left it in the van somewhere. We never found the source of the bad smell until we got to the tabernacle. The wife of our interpreter pulled out a paper sack with fish in it. When she did magnets fell out as she clipped it to a line to hang it out in the sun and covered it with lemon juice said to be a killer of any bacteria. That fish is what she cooked us for dinner that night. Belinda and I, of course, ate our can of soups we brought.

A couple of nights into the revival, a little man came barefoot and worn out clothes. He was a missionary and had been traveling all over Mexico to tell people about Jesus. My dad prayed with him and felt like hugging him and in a brotherly hug they both wept. Not knowing that this little man would have his life taken because of speaking about Jesus after we went back home to the States.

It was a crisp December morning as I went to shower. But not like we had back home in the States. It was just four walls of sheet metal and a water hose that spewed cold water! Later, I watched the interpreter's wife wash clothes in a big pot. I saw the water before anything was put in it, and could see tails wiggling in it! Then I understood why we had to buy drinking water in bottles at the market.

We traveled down to Port Angel on the oceanfront. On the way, dad hit a rock and it put a hole in our oil pan. Well, that was a dilemma. Dad hitchhiked into a village, the only one with a gas station, to buy oil. In Mexico, they take siesta time very seriously. So needless to say, Dad had to wait on the gas station attendants to wake up. After returning to us Dad put a quart of oil into the van. He said he felt something tell him to recheck the oil. It was one quart over full!

There was to be a big feast for us and many of the church women gathered in the yard where the wash basin and shower were and the chickens ran wild with the dogs and pigs. I walked by and a woman reached down in front of me and grabbed a chicken, wringing its neck to kill it. Then she dipped the chicken in water and began to pull its feathers out to prepare for cooking. It was quite a commotion. The happy talking and laughter among the women filled the air.

We went to see the sights of Oaxaca. We went into a Catholic church in the area that was layered in gold inside. I remember how beautiful it was and how sad the statues were of Jesus. I saw a poor little lady that was probably in her seventies put money into a little bowl at the door. She then began to roll up her pants so that her knees were revealed, and she began to crawl around praying as her knees bled. She was desperate for an answer to her prayers. My heart was heavy for her that day.

14

CHAPTER 3

As I walked through the marketplace with my blonde hair, the men would grab my hair and say words I couldn't understand except "bonita," which meant beautiful. I became afraid to leave my dad's side. The interpreter said they thought I was a goddess or an angel because they had never seen light colored hair as mine was golden blonde. Of course, as I grew older my hair changed to light brown then now dark brown, even a few gray hairs thrown in now. I wouldn't trade anything for my experience there, and forever have a love for the peoples of Mexico. In my memory will always be our interpreter Lazarus, and his beautiful wife Chole.

CHAPTER 4

1 John 3:8

My parents began making decisions about our lives that would forever burn in my memory. Dad had a desire to go on the road to take the gospel to other people not just in his church on D street in Ardmore, Oklahoma. While all of this was being thought about, my mother discovered a bug bite or spider bite on her ankle. It grew and became black and rotted deep in the tissue of her ankle. Another appeared on the opposite ankle and did the same thing. Rotting and burning from infection I heard her say, "God will heal me." Other ladies in the church told her things like, "Oh Sister Wood, you will probably lose your leg! You will be crippled for life!" So many things that were negative. But my mom held on to her faith. She knew if God healed people from death beds and wheelchairs this was a simple thing for Him to heal her. With her faith she bought a new pair of red high heel shoes! She wore those shoes! God healed her and she still rejoices today about it.

While my dad was working to set up our gospel tent he stepped out of the bus and when his foot hit the ground it popped very loudly. He was unable to walk and my mom helped to see him to bed, and he rested for several days. Everyone that saw it said it was broken but dad refused to go to a doctor. I heard him every day praying, asking God to heal him. He quoted the scripture, "It was for this purpose the son of God was manifested that he might destroy the works of the devil." 1 John 3:8 (KJV)

One day while he was lying in bed, my grandfather came over to bring crutches for my dad to use. My dad said take them back I won't need them God will heal me! My grandfather said I will set them against the wall just in case. Those crutches never got used! My father started praying again and quoting scripture while moving his foot. Popping sounds came from his ankle as he moved his foot thanking

God with every movement. The next thing I knew my dad had picked up the crutches and carried them to my grandfather's house singing, "Praise The Lord! Hallelujah!" My grandfather was in shock when dad walked into his home and said thank you here are your crutches, I told you I wouldn't need them! Well, Dad and Mom had pretty much decided this was sign enough to sell out and go on the road. They were still holding on taking their time since my sister and I were in school and Dad owned several houses and had a successful painting and drywall business along with our church that was growing.

We attended a tent revival in Oklahoma City that summer. The preacher was R.W. Schambauch. We grew to love this man and his ministry and was sad when he left this world in 2012. He was an amazing man and one that my dad's ministry mirrored. During that service worshipping God with thousands of people the sweet Hammond organ filled the air with jubilant music. The rain began to fall, and you could hear it on the tent and see in come through by the lights at the top of the tent poles. These tent poles were basically telephone poles or what most know as electric poles. The wind hit and the tent canvas moved wildly.

Soon the lights went out and I saw Bro. Schambauch and the others on the stage quickly ran to get under the stage for safety. The poles hit the ground by being lifted with the wind and hitting the ground like a mad elephant. We didn't realize a tornado had hit and the tent began to fall and collapse as people screamed out. I remember the taste of dirt in my mouth as my dad grabbed me and put me on his back. We walked and then crawled out of the side of the tent. There were screams and people helping people find lost loved ones or friends. We left there that night and were amazed no one that we knew of lost their life.

One morning out of the blue a phone call came as I was getting ready to go to second grade class at Jefferson Elementary School. I heard my dad say, "Hello?" He said, "Sure, just a minute." Then he called to me, "Dee Dee!" That is my nickname. I went to him and he said I had a call, that a lady asked to speak to me. I picked up the phone and said, "Hello?" She began to scream at me. She claimed I had pushed her son on the playground and tore his jacket. I didn't know what she was talking about. The boy she mentioned was nice to me and we played together but never had a fuss. She proceeded to call me nasty names, some I won't even say. She then threatened to meet me at school when my parents were not around and cut me up in pieces. She would kill me. This really terrified me, and Dad took the phone as I cried in horror. That was my last day in public school. From then on, I was homeschooled.

Dad saw these two events as proof he needed to take us out of school and hit the road with the gospel!

My dad bought a Shasta travel trailer and said we were going to have revivals. About the third place I remember having a tent revival was in Madill, Oklahoma. Wow, what a great revival! There were two women who were blind, each one of them in one eye only. They could not see anything but darkness. My dad had spent days praying and fasting for God to move. He told God that if the Bible was true and God did miracles then he expected God to show up and do it for us.

I know it sounds crazy, but my dad had amazing faith. You know in the Bible it said when Jesus prayed for a blind eye He used His spit and made mud to put on the blind person's eye? Well, dad took his handkerchief out of his pocket and spit on it. Yes, that is what I said, he spat on the handkerchief and laid it on the woman's eye. He prayed in the name of Jesus, "Eye! Be healed!" She started saying she could see it was light she started seeing! Then he kept saying, "In the name of Jesus eye I command you to be made whole! To be healed!" That lady went home seeing clearly that night! People were there to testify she had been blind a long time.

Chapter 4

The next night, the other lady who was blind came forward to pray. She had heard that God had healed a blind eye the night before. Dad did the same for her. Used his handkerchief and prayed the same prayer. Guess what? She too got healed! I saw these happen right before me!

Another night, there was a woman who came to get delivered from an evil spirit. Well, dad was prepared for this too. She came up for prayer, dad began to pray, and it was not long that the lady began to moan and scream. She laid down and dad put his hand on her head. As he did, she screamed louder and a voice, not like hers, began to cry out and told my dad he wasn't leaving this woman. A lump swelled in her stomach and we watched it move into her throat as the voice said, "I will kill her!" Dad spoke even more boldly and after using the power of Jesus, he did leave her, and she was happy and relieved after the devil had left her.

Denton, Texas. It was hot summertime. I was not playing the drums yet, so I sat with my mom during the services. One night a lady drove up in a car and jumped out screaming that she needed Jesus. Everyone prayed with her and she left happy that night. I remember sitting up in my top bunk bed in that little travel trailer entertaining my young niece Gwyn. She was named after my sisters and me. She was so cute and brought great joy to our family.

We were invited to a brush arbor meeting in Cleveland, Oklahoma. I was curious to see what in the world that was. Well, they had taken four poles and made a roof of tree branches and brush. So, that is why it was called a brush arbor. My dad preached and so did another preacher or two that week or two of revival. We again, saw a great revival. One night, the Lord was moving, people were worshipping and I saw this; It was a fine mist like a cloud coming in over the whole congregation. It was just such a sweet feeling. You knew right off it was God's presence. While the worship leaders sang I and some others heard voices like angels singing along. I still get chill bumps today thinking of it.

21

The next revival, as I recall, was in Hugo, Oklahoma. We were staying in our little travel trailer. I had the bunk bed. The one above the full-size bed my parents slept on. I was not used to being up high and I was awakened by a blunt hit to my head. I had fallen out of bed while turning over. Needless to say, when we got our bus my dad built my bed to be the one on the lower bunk.

One night a preacher my dad had met a couple of years earlier stopped in at our trailer before church service. He asked dad if he could preach and so dad knowing he was a pretty good guy let him do the preaching that night. Well, after worship we all got seated and this man began to talk and I am still not sure what it was all about but he quickly began to yell and kick several chairs over as he screamed. I believe he had been discouraged and hurt by people and didn't know how to deal with it. I remember him and my dad having a long talk. Needless to say that was probably the last time we saw that man. Dad told me all preachers are just men. They fail and they get hurt sometimes. They will let you down, but God never will.

CHAPTER 5

My dad had put our little tent up in Ardmore and we were having service as a man walked in with a pipe wrench. He was screaming with threats to my dad. He said, "Preacher if you don't shut this revival down I will!" Hitting his palm of his hand with the pipe wrench he said, "Shut it down now! You are disturbing my peace." He was drunker than a skunk my dad said later. But, dad, in his kind way went to the man and said sir, "Can I pray for you?" He said he didn't want dad to but then he changed his mind. He fell to his knees and cried for God to save his soul. He stood up a bit and was sober. He asked my dad to follow him home to tell his wife what God had done. My daddy didn't hesitate one bit. He followed this man up the alley way to his back door. The man opened the screen door and called out, "Mama! Come here I have the preacher man with me, and you won't believe what God has done!" In a few minutes, my dad returned with this man and his wife. She was ready to pray too. That night that couple gave their hearts to God and a change really took place in their lives. As far as I know, they lived the rest of their years for Christ.

One night, I saw a large man that had brought his little boy up to my dad for prayer. He had a built-up shoe on and they said one of his legs were shorter than the other. I stood there in awe and praying as my dad spoke to this boy's leg. He said, "Leg, in the name of Jesus be whole. Leg, in the name of Jesus I command you to be healed, to be normal." With my own eyes I saw this little boy's leg begin to grow out. I know it was at least three to four inches shorter than the other. What excitement filled the air! Everyone that was there saw it. God's miraculous power was shown again!

Tishomingo, Oklahoma. We put our tent up in a field there. The one thing I remember mostly about that revival, is one night a lady brought her little daughter for prayer. Her daughter would have epileptic seizures and no doctors could help her. Her daughter went into a seizure during the service and the lady asked dad to please pray for her. That night that little girl was healed! She lived a normal life from then on!

Our first bus was a school bus painted green! I was about seven years old. We were just taking to the bus life. Dad would sometimes park it in between revivals at a lake or a river. This time we parked at Lake Murray in Ardmore, Oklahoma. It was raining and my Dad and I got our fishing poles and headed to the water to catch some fish. The rain patted down on the hood of my little jacket and the cool breeze brushed against my face. I still remember it like yesterday. His laughing, the ducks quacking as they flew by while mom prepared dinner on her little propane stove. Dad had purchased a Greyhound bus when I was eight years old, my mom, sisters and I helped Dad refurbish it. I had so much fun helping him. We stripped out the seats and cleaned it really well. Dad wired it for electricity and put in a septic tank for our bathroom. My sister Belinda and I had bunk beds. I took the lower bunk as I hated being closed in so the window by my bed was nice to have. We put in wall studs, even insulation then paneling. I loved the fluorescent lighting and still do.

Kentucky bluegrass! Well, I didn't think it was blue at all. That silver eagle bus cruised right through the Kentucky Derby area and into Indiana, Ohio, and back into Kentucky stopping at a little mining town named Nortonville. We were so excited; it was our first time to be at this little church. The first night, there were a lot of people and excitement because the youth were having a harvest festival. Everyone dressed up as some kind of Bible or movie character except for me. My sister Belinda curled her hair and made an interesting hairdo like a seventies rock star, I haven't seen her in that costume since.

The people of Kentucky were very kind and friendly to us Oklahomans. They took us in like we were family and fed us every night and brought groceries and Pepsi. Yes, Pepsi! They would leave it at the bus door for us.

One night, we were given a beautiful green tapioca cake. It sat in the fridge for days as we were always being taken out to eat. Well, about a week went by and we decided to finally try that green cake.

It was as fresh as the first day it was brought, and no one was brave enough to eat it. We found out later, a man who owned the local funeral home made it and we were told he used embalming fluid to make his baked goods stay fresh. I have not eaten a piece of green tapioca cake since.

If you have ever attended a real Pentecostal service, then you know that things can get pretty lively. The Lord was moving, and people were shouting and praising God with hands in the air and I was playing my drums. Well, I was giving it all I could and being blessed by watching people getting their blessings when all of a sudden, my drum stool decided to come undone! I fell backwards and when I did my arm hit the light switch and turned out all the stage lights! People thought the Lord really moved on me!

Whatever God has, the devil has a counterfeit. During this revival one night, my Dad was preaching, and he began to do the thing with his hand. He had told us that if we ever saw him moving his hand while preaching in a waving motion at his side it was because he felt his angel. Dad's hand was really going and about that time a man got down on the floor behind where I was sitting and swerved just like a snake through people's feet under the pews! When he came out at the front my Dad and the Pastor grabbed him and began to pray. He was delivered from demons that night and came to the rest of the revival a changed man.

I was baptized on that trip in Nortonville, Kentucky by Pastor Gunn. I had my tenth birthday that week also. My dad called me up to the stage to sing and since it was my birthday, they took up an offering that totaled $100 while I sang a song! I felt so good, that was the first time I had received money for singing. I laid on my bunkbed in our Greyhound bus counting it over and over. My dad said that made me a professional singer. I thought that was great!

Kentucky became a regular place for us to have revival. Every Easter we went there. I made a lifelong friend there. She became like my sister. Her name is Theresa I will use her maiden name here, Rickard. Some people come into your life and then are gone. Some are angels who come and throughout your life even though you are apart you sometimes feel the flutter of their wings because they are so special.

It was fall and the breeze was cool. There was a tractor and trailer beside the cutest little country church in the beautiful hills of Kentucky. I fell in love with the people and the area. I even talked of moving there when I turned eighteen. Of course, I never did because I couldn't risk breaking my mom and dad's heart. But I enjoyed every moment I was able to be there.

The tractor puttered through the dark road and into the cemetery where unbeknownst to us my daddy had hidden behind some tombstones. As we rode through, I was sitting by my friends and a young farm boy I had a crush on. Dad jumped out and scared us so bad. We all screamed and needless to say, I was very embarrassed.

Teresa's family were tobacco farmers and during the day I got to spend the day with them. They became like family to me. Douglas, her father, was so funny and he kept us kids laughing. Barbara, her mother, was so kind and quiet but when she spoke you listened. I only heard her speak up when what she had to say was important. I got to ride on the big green tractor! Rushing through the field disking up the dirt to plant their crop for that year. Beautiful scenes of a hill of trees and I felt the dirt blow into my face and the sun burn my skin. The boy who was driving was Paul, Teresa's brother. Then the next day or say I got to ride on the back of a smaller tractor and watch the seeds be planted that later grew into a huge harvest. To this day, I know I have a home if needed. I know I can go to Kentucky and be loved just as much as I was then. Priceless are those relationships and I will cherish them until I die.

Later, back in Arkansas, my dad was preaching a revival in Fort Smith, Arkansas. One night, he preached on the sword of the Lord.

How we use our faith to fight the devil and he demonstrated how you take the sword and stab the devil. So, after church I was playing with other kids when this boy about twelve years old, came up pretending to fight with a sword and he accidently hit my left eye. Blood began to flow down my face, and I lost sight in that eye. I ran into the church crying and immediately. I believe God healed me. I gained my sight back with no scar or damage to my eye. Later, in my twenties, I went for an eye exam and the doctor couldn't believe I had recovered. But, I know it was God.

In the same town later, we parked our bus out by a little cinder block church where a friend of ours was holding a revival. One night, after service storms began to roll in. My dad, mom, sister, and I were in the travel trailer of our friends who were preaching there. Eating sandwiches, talking, and laughing the trailer began to really shake. My dad remembered the bus windows were open. He opened the door on the trailer and stuff was flying in the air. the lights went out and dad hollered hit the floor! We all got down and I felt that trailer lift off the ground! It lifted and slammed down at least three times. As soon as it stopped the preacher opened the door and said run to the church now! As I placed my bare foot onto the metal step and next into ankle deep water a ball of electricity came rolling down the road in the water from downed power lines! Run! Run! I heard my dad say. We rode the storm out and we survived again!

It was a cold morning in Cleveland, Oklahoma and Dad was never one to ask for money. He didn't like taking up offerings and said God will provide. We had been in revival, but our money was low, and we had run out of propane overnight. So, when I rolled over my bed covers were frozen to the wall of the bus by my bunk bed. I still remember the sound as I pulled them away from the wall and saw my breath in the air. I cuddled deeper into my covers and tried to stay warm in my fuzzy socks I got in Mexico. At that moment, I knew whenever I got out on my own, I would have a central heat and air unit.

A very boisterous preacher woman came into our town and became friends with our family that lasted many years. She was known for a song she had written called "Holy Roller." She was a large woman who shook a tambourine like she meant business. She could look you in the eye and you felt she could read every thought you had. Even though she could be very intimidating, she could also be loving. Her hopes were I would grow up and marry her son. He was a good friend, but we never went the path of love. Her name was Sister Parker and her husband she called Daddy, He was actually named Ray. He painted houses for a living and one time he was painting in a house and didn't know that a hot water heater was still lit. There was a horrible explosion as the fumes from the paint filled the air. Ray was burned very badly and lost one of his ears. I went with my parents to visit him and I remember the smell his body emitted. He was surely in a lot of pain and I almost couldn't stand to see him. He had dad pray for him to be healed. He said God could heal him and

I believed he would. So, dad laid hands on him and prayed that his body would be healed. The next time we saw him a few months later he was better, and he had a brand-new ear! Yes! A new ear! I had to walk up close to see it and it was fresh new skin with cartilage! God did it again!

Duncan, Oklahoma. We were attending a revival of a friend. As my mom sat through the service the Lord impressed upon her heart to give the evangelist a bag of groceries. She made her way out into our bus and began bagging up can goods. She knew what it was like to travel and preach the gospel and have needs that no one else understood. As she dug through the cans of vegetables the one can of corn kept catching her eye. She said Lord, you know my family loves corn and I can't give it away. But, again she couldn't shake off the feeling of giving that lone can of corn away. Ever since that night my mom has yet to ever be without a can of corn. Whether it is from a church donation to her as a widow or family bringing in extras, she says to this day she always has corn.

I haven't mentioned yet but in the times we put up the tent for a revival us girls helped dad to lay out the tent, lace it up, slide the poles under it and put the stakes along with each rope. Putting up the tent was hard work but we didn't mind because we knew that God was going to do something great!

Dad had located an empty lot then went to city hall to get permission to use it. Dad carried an electric pole with us then would get an electric permit and the city would connect it. We then had electricity for the lights, music equipment, and our bus. Mom would make strawberry milkshakes and we would go in the bus to cool ourselves and rest before finishing the task of putting the tent in the air.

The air was musty and hot in Wichita Falls as my brother-in-law, Lavoy, led the worship and started the service as dad's front man. Lavoy is married to my oldest sister Sheila. He had given his heart to God in a revival we had in Madill, Oklahoma. A Chickasaw native with long black hair won my sister's heart. They have three wonderful children: one girl and a set of twins.

Back to my night in Wichita Falls revival was happening as God was moving! Night after night there had been testimony of the miracles. One really stands out in my memory of a mother who had an adult daughter that had been put into the mental hospital not knowing who she was or where she was. So, the mother came for prayer to stand in for her daughter asking God to restore her mind. Dad anointed a prayer cloth and gave it to the mom to take and put in her daughter's room. A few days later the mother came to us to tell us what God had done! She said she walked in the room to see her daughter and the daughter was brushing her hair looking in a mirror and said to her mother, "Hello I am glad you are here mom." The Lord had restored her mind and she recognized her mother right away!

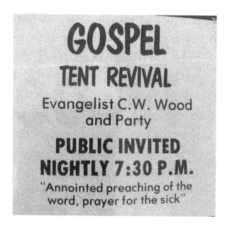

During the day, while Dad spent time in prayer, I would spend time under the tent. I would pretend to preach, and I had many great revivals all by myself. But this time I had made a friend, Sarah she lived not too far down the road and we would spend time talking and laughing. The dirt flew up into my sandals as we walked to the little store on the corner. You know the kind, like in a 1950's movie. The screen door would screech as it opened, and the air was filled with music as an old man greeted us. We reached our hands into a barrel of cold root beer floating in ice and water. Grabbing a candy bar and paying as we headed back out the screeching screen door.

One night during service, there came a man all dressed up in a nice white suit. He had at least four young women with him. Two women sat on each side of him and wiped his face with handkerchiefs. He had long fingernails and was very scary to me. Apparently, he ran that neighborhood and was known as an Apostle of God. Well, I am not so sure it was my God he represented, but he sure put on a show. He came back several times during revival repeating where he sat and the women with him. On this night, he walked in as my dad started to preach. Right in front of me and everyone, he walked up to my dad and said, "Hey, preacher what if I just shoot you through?" Dad said, "Well, I guess you just have to do what you have to do." I was so afraid and started praying in my mind. For some reason, he backed away from my dad and left. He didn't come back that night.

As we slept in our bus that was parked by the tent, we had our Doberman pinscher dog guarding all our equipment under the tent. I was awakened from my sleep in the bus with a strange man banging his hands on the side of the bus. Screaming something about he was God and he was going to call fire down on us. Seems I remember my brother in law saying, "Man, where do these people come from?" The man only stayed long enough to scare us and then he went on his way down the street.

We had been invited to hold a revival in Little Rock, Arkansas. Things were going pretty well, but the revival was not taking off as well and we were low on money for food and gas. One day out of the blue, this beautiful Lincoln Continental pulled into the parking lot and pulled up to the bus. It was our Greyhound bus that dad had painted a flame down each side. I loved that bus and my little cozy bunk bed. This car pulled up and a man in a suit got out and knocked on the bus door. Dad answered him and the man said he felt like God told him to stop and give us $100. He went on his way and we never saw him again. God knew we had a need and used this man to bless us.

One of the revivals we held was in Fouke, Arkansas. If you know where that is, I am impressed! The pine trees were tall, and the smell of fall filled the air. I remember as we drove up to this little white church a very tall man waiting for us. Dad drove the bus right in beside the church, and we all got out. The tall man introduced himself as Long Legs and that was no understatement, he was very tall.

The forest was all around us and out from the church was an old cemetery. I helped unload our music equipment and mostly carried in my drums and set them up getting ready for church. That night people began to come up and park in the little dirt parking lot. The church was packed with people. My sister and I sang songs with dad and by ourselves. The people loved to hear us sing our Spanish songs we had learned while in Old Mexico.

The revival was going really well, but one night someone cut many of the car tires. We were told someone in the community was angry about the church doing well. That just made these folks want more of what God had for them.

There was an old story about how there was a Bigfoot monster who lived around there in the forest. It was the Fouke Monster, and someone even gave us a book about the monster. Needless to say, my imagination went wild. I thought I heard a scream in the woods just like they claimed the monster made. I tried to not be outside alone after that.

My sister Theresa decided to join us. She and her husband had a Volkswagen bus that was also a camper. One morning they told us that during the night something actually shook the camper. My brother-in-law said he looked but didn't see anything. He was later told it was probably the Fouke monster because he had done that to others. It is still a mystery today what it was.

When traveling, we had to heat our hot water on the stove and pour it into a plastic wash pan to wash our dishes. I remember using a hand towel to dry them and put them away as I talked with my mom. I enjoyed those days and wouldn't trade any of the memories.

Summertime in Locust Grove, Oklahoma we put up the tent. Many people came and God moved. Souls were saved and hearts mended. One little elderly lady who was known to be very wealthy took a liking to my dad. She told him to go down to the boot store and tell them she had sent him. She said she had already paid for him a pair of boots and all he had to do was tell the clerk and he could pick them out. My dad went down to the boot store and told them she sent him, and they said, "Oh yes! She paid for you a pair of boots." Any that he wanted for $200! In the early 80's that was a nice pair of boots for that price!

Dad had been reading in the Bible in John 5; 1-9 about the pool of Bethesda. It was a pool in Jerusalem that Jesus used to heal a paralyzed man. The angel troubled the water and Jesus told the man to enter and he would be healed. Dad told us I know it sounds crazy, but I feel God is in this. So, he bought a child's pool, filled it with water and he placed it right in front of the stage where people always came for prayer. As dad preached about the pool of Bethesda and how the waters were stirred, he encouraged people to step in and receive their miracle. I saw many people start to put their first foot in and they said it felt like electricity when they touched the water. They would proceed to stand in the water as Dad prayed for them. You could sense the power of God as many people began to cry and raise their hands in rejoicing. There were many who were healed and delivered.

Well, one night during service the storms began to blow in. Another tornado was predicted by the weatherman. Dad said we will be fine. We are having church anyway. So as the worship music started, and people began to praise God the wind really picked up. I remember the wind getting stronger and my mom and brother-in-law started to lower the tent sides to help keep the tent in place. I soon saw my dad step out from under the tent. I wasn't playing music with my sisters, so I joined him. I watched as my dad rebuked the storm. Yes, he spoke to the storm. He said, "Peace be still! I command it in the name of Jesus! Storm you have to listen to me for I have authority in the Jesus name!" Immediately, the winds began to calm down the tornado they said was coming had dissipated and the clouds actually parted right before my eyes! We went on with revival and later after we had taken down the tent and was gone people told us a tornado came right through where the tent had been and damaged many buildings in the area.

While traveling, dad would often try to find a place to park our bus that he felt was safe for us to sleep. One particular night, I remember we had parked in a town we were not really familiar with and we pulled the curtains and locked up. As we all got into our beds, we lay there like the Waltons did, saying good night and all. Suddenly, a very loud train horn sounded, and I asked, "Dad did you park us on a train track?" He said, "No." Then Mom said, "Honey, are you sure you didn't park us on a train track?" He said, "No." He got up to check and the train went by about that time with quite a rumble.

Another time, we parked by a river in Hugo, Oklahoma and there was a dam. Dad parked us on the lower end so he and I could fish while mom cooked supper. After our fishing and eating we all made it into our beds and laid there again like the Waltons, and then suddenly, sirens started sounding! Dad said, "Oh, that is nothing, just letting people know the dam gates were opening up." My sister asked, "Dad you didn't park us in the wrong place, did you?" He said, "No, we are fine." Thankfully, we were but the river rose pretty close that night.

Then we were somewhere around Chicago or Cincinnati and Dad got sleepy, so he pulled us in by a little side road and we all crawled in our beds and said our Walton exchanges and all of the sudden, a huge airplane flew right over us and shook the bus! Mom said, "Honey you didn't park us on an air strip, did you?" He said, "No, we are fine." The next morning, we realized we were at the very end of an air strip! I know it sounds like we didn't trust Dad, but we did.

We were holding a revival in Waco, Texas and when it would rain my sisters and I would catch rainwater in a bucket that came off of the tent to wash our hair in. The rainwater would make your hair soft and shiny. Since water had to be conserved for drinking in our water tank on the bus, we would go swim in the local lake or river. We would take a bar of soap and lather up and watch the suds float away. We bathed in the water with our clothes on but you know it was so much fun trying to keep people from seeing what we were doing while we laughed so hard because it was a challenge indeed.

On the way home to Oklahoma from a revival in San Antonio, the brakes went out on the bus right as we hit the Fort Worth rush hour traffic. Mom was driving the pickup truck pulling our trailer which had our gospel tent in it and dad told her to stay close he was going to have to keep the bus moving. The Lord kept us safe and we made it.

Another time, I remember dad said, "You guys pray." I woke up as I had been sleeping while we traveled. We had been in Louisiana in revival at a pastor friends church. I asked what was wrong and Dad said we are running out of gas and may not make it. There were no gas stations, and it was very dark except for our lights on the bus. We prayed and we drove on empty making our destination. Again, God came through.

We were headed to Canada in winter one year and there was a minister who promised he would meet us there for Dad to preach a revival. On our way up we took a little time to visit the tourist attractions at Custer's Battlefield and it was very heartbreaking to me. Later in the evening, the minister we were meeting suggested we visit a little Native American church. As the people strolled in, so did we. No one spoke to us and stared intently at us which was extremely uncomfortable. We were on reservation land and never had been there and did not know anyone. After they sang the worship songs, the pastor of the little church went up and began to preach. Remember, we had not been acknowledged at this point. He was preaching how God can change you and he said, "If I was not a Christian, these people would not be sitting here with their scalps on!" Wow, very scary to a young girl like me. I wish I had known at that time that I would descend from Chief Pushmataha. He is my eighth great-grandfather on my Dad's side and Pocahontas is my eleventh great grandmother on my mother's side.

After we spent the night there in our bus, we moved on to Casper, Wyoming where a Pastor awaited us for service. We traveled through the mountains and saw a lot of antelope and beautiful scenery with nothing around for miles.

Our bus began to make a rattling sound and Dad pulled over to check things out. He told us that the motor was only being held up by one bolt! Nowhere to get it fixed and no money really to do so. We prayed and drove on. As we approached Casper it was getting dark and Dad found a place to pull the bus over and we all got settled into our beds. Our bus had the words Jesus Saves with a cross on the very back. Apparently, some people did not like it. As we lay trying to sleep a pickup truck drove by with guys screaming out loud and throwing beer bottles on the back of the bus where the sign was.

The next day there was clear blue sky and very cold. It was winter in Casper, Wyoming. We found the church where we were to hold service. We got ready for service and walked into a beautiful sanctuary. They passed around communion after worship and as we started to take it my mom stopped me. She said don't drink it then said ok go ahead. The was the strangest grape juice I ever had in communion! It was wine they served which was new to me. The crowd this time was all white people with an awesome African-American pastor and a sweet wife. As we got to know them after service, and they treated us to a meal in a nice restaurant.

CHAPTER 5

Our plans changed after Dad received word through the pastor that the minister we were meeting, was not going to meet us in Canada after all. We were left with going back home. We headed south with a blue norther headed south too. We drove hard to make it one to Oklahoma before that snowstorm could catch us.

I was taught to simply ask if I had a need. God would help me no matter what. I am so thankful to have been taught this by my parents.

CHAPTER 6

I John 4:4

The summer breeze was softly blowing as my dad began to preach. This night mosquitoes were bad. I grabbed the can of repellent and sprayed my ankles and feet as I had sandals on, my favorite summer shoes. We had just had an awesome worship service and I had sat down beside my mom. After settling into my chair ready to hear dad preach, I heard going by ear a loud whiz sound and *Ting*! Mom said, "Did you hear that? It sounded like a bullet." We listened and watched cars driving by to see if we heard or saw anything else. After the service, we looked around and sure enough a bullet had come by my head and hit the bus door! I couldn't believe that had come so close to my head. I could have died!

A few years later in Shawnee, Oklahoma, we had another amazing tent revival. Seeing many delivered from demons or being healed. My sister Theresa and her husband had driven up to see us again but, this time pulling a new AirStream travel trailer. After the service, my parents, my sister Belinda, and I went into their travel trailer to see it and visit. I decided to sit on the floor playing with my two nieces as my family visited at the table. While I was sitting there, I can still remember the sound of the car squealing its tires and a loud *Bang*! All of a sudden, glass above my head shattered and fell all around me. Once again, I had missed a bullet and gave God glory for His protection.

The warm breeze hit my face as I adjusted my hair and followed my dad along with my mother and my sisters into a little church. Dad had his guitar and amp in his hands as he walked up to the stage where he had been invited to preach. My mom, sisters, and I sat down and were greeted by people with handshakes. The crowd seemed to be very friendly. As the piano player started playing and the crowd began to sing, I was singing along and clapping my hands when things took a weird turn. I noticed an old lady sitting across the aisle from me. Her fingers began to crinkle up and she started speaking out very loudly. She started saying things like, "You and your family will die. You will not make it home tonight." At this point, my Dad was seeing and hearing this. The pastor decided he didn't want Dad to preach and Dad came quickly with his guitar and said let's go. We quickly left because we were not wanted, and Dad would not stay when the pastor didn't want us there. We all were troubled by what had just happened and talked about why this happened; we didn't even know any of these people. On the way out, someone had told Dad this old lady was a witch and was trying to place a curse on us. This memory has stayed in my mind all these years.

Tulsa, Oklahoma. Revival season was beginning again. The Hammond organ, drums, bass guitar, and dad's guitar were sounding through that hot summer night. A woman came up after Dad's preached and wanted prayer for her daughter, who was deaf and mute. Dad asked what she needed, and she said, "I want God to heal my daughter." I remember the command my Dad gave, he said, "Ear, in the name of Jesus, I command you to be healed." Then he would whisper into her ears and repeated several times saying, "Ear be healed! In the name of Jesus be healed!" Then he did something that would seem crazy. He told the girl to say, "Baby." He spoke into her ear changing right to left side. "Ear! I command you to be healed!" Then said the word "Baby." After a few more times she said it! She said, "Baby!" She was so excited and started crying. God healed her! She and I became friends and we stayed in touch with letters for many years until life took us into other directions.

Muskogee, Oklahoma. We were having a great revival, and one night after service I had already gone into the bus. I heard a lady speaking loudly and my dad's voice. I knew something was not right. I looked out the curtain over the window by my bunk bed in our Greyhound bus. I could see my mom and dad talking to this woman who was threatening to throw matches into her gas tank. She was trying to blow us up and she was apparently in need of help. My dad began to calm her down and they prayed with her and gave her heart to Jesus that night.

A small country church in Madill, Oklahoma a creaking wooden floor the little preacher was a woman with gray hair and glasses. She was spunky and had a big heart. Her name was Sister Hale. The music played as I walked into service and sat beside my childhood friend, and still close friend, Connie Cryer. My brother-in-law, Lavoy's, sister. As I sat down, the pinch on my leg from the wooden bench was hard to overlook as I sat down. She filled me in on what I had missed, and the worship began. Sister Hale had a voice that could be heard outside the building as she worshipped God. The fans were blowing the air as people began to stand and clap in joyous worship. So many great services in that little church. It is still a church today.

As time went by, my sisters all got married, and I, being the baby of the family, was the only one left at home. On Saturday nights a local little church would have gospel singings. That is where my now husband, Kirk, caught my eye. He was the drummer for The Priddy Family. His folks had a southern gospel band and traveled a lot to different churches. But I always hoped he would be there whenever we were off the road and could attend. I got the opportunity to go along some and sing with the Priddy's. Kirk has a sister named Karen who sings, and she has a voice of an angel. I dated Kirk as a teenager. He was such a practical joker. I laughed so much when I was with him. I didn't know what the future had in store for us many years later. Life took him a different direction as it did me.

We drove up to a little white church as it was getting dark. It was Bull Frog Corner, Mississippi. There was only one little streetlight, as I recall, that lit up the yard. The pastor had told us to make ourselves at home and hook up our bus to electricity and water. When we got out of the bus, Dad realized the key was not where they told us it would be. So, my Dad being the handy man he was, took it upon himself to pick the lock. He did and got the church door open. He found the electric hookup and we were set. Since it was still a little light in the sky I explored with my sister and we saw an old cemetery beside the church. It was full of graves that were one hundred to two hundred years old! Most of them were broken open and you could see through the lid of the coffins. I saw bones in one and decided that was enough. Needless to say, I didn't sleep very well that night. The next day was Sunday and the church was packed. We had a great service and after I went home with the Pastor's daughter to get acquainted and we stopped at a little store. The Pastor asked, "Do you want anything?" I said, "Sure how about a pop?" He said, "Wait, what did you say?" I repeated myself and he said, "That would be your father, not a drink." I asked what they called it and he said, "Coke or soda water." So I said, "Okay, get me a pop that is coke soda water but says Dr.Pepper."

I was around the age of eighteen, Dad had been a painter on the side when he wasn't preaching, and he had an offer to do a job. It was waterproofing the outside of a building. He sprayed the waterproof as the cold wind blew and he didn't wear protection for his lungs. After that day, he began to develop problems with his lungs. Dad was my buddy, not just my father, and it was hard to watch him go through the beginning of this sickness.

By this time, the popularity of revivals had slowed down, and the church began to modernize. Going from old fashioned worship to contemporary. No longer needing southern gospel or just good ol' gospel music and going from a preaching to a teaching environment. Time was changing, and dad was not able to get bookings anymore. As a result of this, I began to find my own path playing piano, leading worship, speaking at women's ministry services, and doing special singing when invited. I started my own Christian band and had heard of a young saxophone player and a male vocalist who was interested in playing with me. I visited the local church and met them. We decided to practice and get to know each other. That started our short-lived adventure playing in southern Oklahoma and north Texas at Assembly of God, Baptist, Methodist, and Independent churches.

I have been a singer since I was about four years old and I had dreamed about being a star someday. Not even knowing I was related to cousins such as Dolly Parton, Merle Haggard, Patsy Cline, Reba McEntire, June Carter, Whitney Houston, Shania Twain, John Denver, Mickey Gilley, and many others including Michael Jackson! I have found them in researching genealogy. I spent time sending cassette tapes for auditions to many recording studios and one day I received a phone call from one of my favorite gospel singers, Kenny Hinson. He visited with me about an hour on the phone and gave me advice. He also informed me that the days of being offered a contract without paying for it was over. So, I put my singing dream way back on the back burner.

My dad had put our last bus up for sale which brought a lot of lookers wanting to buy our second Silver Eagle. On one visit, a gentleman, who was a producer from Nashville, arrived. Dad had told him that I sing, and he requested I sing a song for him. After I sang the producer said, "If you will sign a contract and go country, I will sign you now." My dad being the preacher he was, just looked at me and shook his head no. I had just turned eighteen and going against dad was not even thinkable. Soon the producer called to speak with me, and he said he wanted me to open for Conway Twitty in Durant, Oklahoma. He asked if I could sing gospel and I said, "Yes." I think Dad must have talked with him because I never heard from him again.

I married the saxophone player in 1986. He was a country boy with French and Native-American heritage. We bought a twenty-five-foot travel trailer right after we married. Not for traveling in ministry like I grew up doing, but for my new husband's job.

We traveled to his jobs from Oklahoma City to Amarillo, Texas ending up for a while in DeSoto, Texas. I had taken a job as a daycare teacher. It was my first real job out in the public sector, I was in for an awakening.

Our first stop was Sands Springs, Oklahoma where my new husband had to work, and we found a little trailer park on the river to stay. I had such a hard time adjusting to my new role. It was right before cell phones or Wi-Fi, so I was completely cut off from family. Craig, my husband, would work many nights as I sat there alone in that trailer in the hot summer with no air conditioner or hot water. When he got home, I would heat water on the stove and pour into the little bathtub then poured onto his head and body to help him bathe. Soon rain set in and it rained for days. We were not able to hook up and move out. One night, he came in and said, "We have to leave. I am supposed to be in Amarillo tomorrow for a job." We frantically found the owner of the park who had a tractor and he pulled our little trailer out of the mud and up onto a dryer spot on the road and we hooked up our vans and headed out that night.

I was a year older than Craig so when we stopped to rent a room to bathe and rest, I had to go in and rent the room because he wasn't old enough. I held that over his head for a long time.

In Amarillo, Craig was there on a job in a beef packing plant. One day, in my little travel trailer, I was washing dishes and getting ready to prepare dinner when I felt a great sadness. Something was wrong. I began to cry and pray that God would enter the situation. I didn't know if it was my family in Oklahoma or my husband, but God was letting me know to pray. Soon a knock came to the door and it was a man Craig worked with. He said Craig was in an accident and needed me at the hospital. I went with him and when I got there, they said he was asking for me by my maiden name Wood. We had only been married three months and I was so scared. I met his doctor; his name was Dr. Hatchet! No joke! While he was talking to me the intercom announced they needed Dr. Hyde! Anyway, his doctor said Craig was caught in a conveyor belt and his legs were pulled between two rollers. About the time I felt the need to pray. If it had gone one more inch up his leg, to his knees, he would have been crippled for life.

After Amarillo, we headed to DeSoto, Texas. We soon found a church to join and helped lead their youth group and filled in with music as needed. Soon, I was offered a public-school job and earned my Title I Teachers Aid certification. I loved my new job and my new life finally adjusting. Through the budget cuts of Texas schools, I had a chance to move on to another school in Lewisville. We moved our little trailer which we soon sold and bought a thirty-five-foot trailer with two tip outs. I felt we had really moved up town. Not to mention we had central heat and air. Something I had dreamed of a long time. That meant no more frozen covers or seeing your breath in the air while sleeping.

God has always used dreams in my life to help me or warn me. One night, I dreamed electric wires were coming out of our trailer wall in our bedroom. They were just wiggling and were blue, red, and black. I told Craig about it, and he kind of laughed at me. But when he came home that day, he said that dreams saved his life! He was crawling through an attic and right before he laid his hand down it reminded him of my dream and as he looked down where his hand was going were bare wires that would have shocked him.

I was still playing with the idea of being a singer when I sent in an audition tape to the Grand Ole Opry. I received a letter that they loved my voice and asked if I could come do a live audition. I had sent in Patsy Cline songs and with no experience or professional guidance I decided to do more modern country for my audition. So, I chose Wynonna Judd songs. I still admire her and love her music. We flew to Nashville from Dallas and stayed in the Opryland Hotel. It was so amazing. I got up early and prepared my songs for the audition. After I met the person in a room behind the Opry and I sang he said, "Well, we love your voice, but maybe next time because we liked your

Patsy Cline but not the new songs." I did not get another chance to do anything different, so I flew home disappointed.

We were attending Freedom Christian Center when one night the Lord had really been moving. The people were in the alters praying and weeping like the presence of God was all around. We just worshiped Him and felt His sweetness in our hearts. I finished praying and the pastor had me and another lady go up to sing while people were praying. I didn't know it, but that lady would be my lifelong friend. Sheila Burns- we were like sisters in looks and hearts. Soon after, I sang at her and her husband Steve's wedding. We had many camping trips and the birth of my two daughters, Demetria and Alexandria, and her two daughters, Hailey and Hollie, means we still have a wonderful friendship.

We met a couple who had a Texas swing country gospel band known as The Sniders. We made friends and soon became a part of the band. I played the drums and sang lead and background vocals. My husband played saxophone and we performed for many Opry's, festivals, and churches all over Texas, not to mention playing for the Texas Governor's campaign on his ranch. I was honored to win the award for top female drummer in Texas gospel music.

I was enjoying this time in my life. During this time, I received news that my mother's youngest sister had been murdered with her four young children. I went to be with my mom and grandmother and tried to wrap my mind around all that had happened. I cannot share everything with you in this book out of respect for my cousins who survived this tragedy. I laid in bed for about two days with grief.

Soon the band fell apart, as we learned the leader had some personal issues. Even being a Christian, people can fall. He began to show affection for me, and I had shared it with my husband. My husband was hurt after he had trusted this man to be his friend and fellow Christian. My heart felt for his precious wife, whom I had grown to love. We met with our pastor and made the decision to part ways.

Soon my husband's job as a Union member was in danger as the Union was dying out and jobs were going away. He had an offer to move to Missouri where my sister Belinda and her family lived. I had heard my nephew Cameron had been praying we would move up to Missouri. We did around February 1992. My parents were sad to see us leave to go to Missouri, and again I was in for an awakening.

I was not able to keep working in public education as the position of Title I Aide was not available in Missouri, as it was in Texas. It was also lower pay with no benefits. So, I had to start looking for other work. As the days passed, I called my parents every day because I was missing home. The culture shock of Missouri from living in Texas and missing my friends and family was almost unbearable for me except that I was able to be with my sister and her family. Just about every weekend, my two nephews were either staying the night or going somewhere with my husband and me.

I truly grew closer to my two nephews Cameron and Nathan. After they grew up, Nathan opened his own martial arts school after becoming the state champion of Missouri. Cameron earned his Associates Degree in Art and soon started modeling for a local clothing shop.

My husband and I bought a home in McCord Bend, Missouri, a small community on the James river. We had been living there for a week when I got the call from my mom that she needed me. Dad had been taken to the hospital and was not doing very well. I drove down the next day taking my Great Dane puppy for a companion on the long road home. I made it around 4 p.m. that day and went straight to the hospital. I met my mom and said my hello to dad made sure he was comfortable and then took my puppy to their home to settle in for the night. Waking up early to get ready to visit dad and I saw a little sparrow that had somehow gotten in the house. The little bird sat on the ceiling fan and I tried to catch him to put him out of the house, but he disappeared from our view and we went on to the hospital.

Not many days before my dad went into the hospital, he had said to me that he was sorry that I had gone without nice things and had to live in a bus. Because we had little money due to him selling everything and going on the road to preach. I assured my dad as we both cried, I have never regretted my life growing up in a bus and I would not take anything for my experiences. My Dad and mom always showed us girls their love and we were well taken care of. In most people's eyes we were poor but, in mine we were rich.

My dad believed in miracles and I hadn't given up on the fact God could heal my dad if He would. I prayed, I read scripture, and I called everyone I knew that could pray. Dad had peace and trusted God. This was just the day after I had gotten home to see him, and it wasn't long after that he started going downhill. His breathing got worse and the doctor said dad needed a lung transplant or he would die. The transplant was not an option as my parents had no insurance nor enough money to make it happen. So, all we had was our faith. Dad raised up in his bed and like he saw Him, he said, "Jesus! Come on, do what you are going to do?" The doctor soon told my mom and I dad chose to be put on a ventilator and we had to leave the room. We didn't know it was going to be the last time we got to speak to him.

When we were brought into his room, he was unconscious and on the ventilator. We were so sad and upset I tried to be strong for mom and yet I was falling apart. None of my sisters were able to be there. We thought he would get better and we would have him home again with mom. As the night closed in, mom and I went back to their home. When we walked in, we found the little sparrow dead on the couch. As I picked him up and took to the outside garden, I felt this was a sign that my dad wasn't coming back home.

The next day, we drove to the hospital and dad was still on the ventilator, and had made it through the night. There was hope he might pull through, in my mind anyway. After hours of praying and hoping I was standing by my dad's bedside when we heard a very loud boom sound. The electricity went out and while standing by his side I felt a strong wind blow into my face, and I felt my dad had been taken to heaven. No one knew what the loud sound was, maybe the sound was his angel Vision and Revelation that he had seen years ago taking him home. It was then that dad went into cardiac arrest and we lost him. It was 1995, April 23, we lost him to emphysema caused by damage to his lungs linked to his spraying the waterproofing a few years back. Time went on and my mother moved in with my husband and I, after we felt it was the best thing for her.

CHAPTER 7

Psalm 147:3

Before we lost my dad, my husband and I had started having marriage issues no one knew about. He had even asked me to leave the night before I went to Oklahoma to see dad. He said it would be best if we separated before we had children. My heart could not accept what he was saying. I asked if we could talk later about it. At the time, we were youth pastors, and I was a worship leader in a small church in Galena, Missouri. We had what everyone thought was a perfect marriage. I struggled to keep us together and work in the ministry where my heart was. We didn't talk about our marriage issues anymore and moved my mother in trying to help her grieve and also start our family. I spent my days being a housewife, worship leader, youth pastor and trying to keep mom distracted from our problems and her sadness.

We wanted to have children, but it just didn't happen. So, I spent time with exams and tests to see why I couldn't conceive. I wanted children more than anything, yet I couldn't seem to get pregnant. Test after test found no problem, it was just up to God. I was excited when I found out I was pregnant and then learned it was twins. I was about three months along. I went in for my check up and at that doctor's visit, they did a sonogram and one of the twin's hearts had stopped. He told me the other one was fine, but for me to come back in a week. When I went in for the next doctor visit before heading to Oklahoma for my husband's family reunion. The doctor ordered a sonogram and proceeded to tell me the other baby had also passed. No heartbeat was found, he took me into the hospital, and I went through a DNC immediately. I had not felt such sadness before. Knowing my babies were gone and I just gave up on having a child ever.

A revival like I hadn't seen in years since my youth broke out. It was in Brownsville, Florida. I didn't go, but people in our little church did and brought back that revival fire with them. The little Assembly of God caught on fire for God! We normally ran around fifty people in attendance, but soon we were running a hundred or more. They brought in busloads of people and raised the windows so people outside could hear! The altars were full every night and God was moving. The pastor requested that an evangelist come preach a revival. Bro. Webb was his name. He was a tall well-dressed man who spoke with power and authority just like my dad. The power of God showed up! That little church had a wooden floor with a basement under it and when those people started shouting that floor moved!

Articles were written about our church in the Assembly of God's Evangel magazine part of the Assemblies of God. We soon had a crowd of up to two and three hundred people. This little country church had busses pulling in and windows raised so all could hear the singing and preaching. God healed people, saved souls, restored families and I was on cloud nine. Soon the pastor put a stop to the revival. Questioning if it was real and sent the evangelist home. My heart was saddened, and my husband said no more. He would never go to a Pentecostal church again, He was done. And our lives changed after that.

I went to another revival service in Branson, Missouri about forty minutes from my home. I had put my offering in that night when the preacher said, "As you place your offering in the plate, remind God of what you want." I told God I wanted a baby. My heart was empty after my miscarriage and I wanted my child if it was His will. About two months after that night, I dreamed my dad handed me a baby girl with dark hair he had wrapped in a pink blanket. He said I am done playing with her now you can have her. I realized I needed to take a test and my doctor confirmed I was two months pregnant from the night I prayed to God with my offering.

I was so excited about my baby that God had given me and would soon get to hold. I was in labor over twenty-four hours with Demetria and while I was in labor, she was turned wrong. The doctor said if she doesn't turn, we will have to do a c-section. Something I didn't want, so I asked my sister Belinda to pray. I knew God would help me. As Belinda prayed, she laid her hand on my stomach and asked God to make Demetria turn to the correct position. Immediately she flipped and it took my breath away. When he came back the doctor was amazed that she had done so. I had a healthy delivery thanks to God.

Soon we moved on to a Baptist church as my husband wanted to try something different. After visiting with the Baptist pastor, I was won over by his knowledge and kindness. He assured me it was not looked down on me to be filled with the Holy Ghost, he just asked me to keep it in my personal prayer time, not in church. I was desperate to save my marriage, so I was okay with it. The people made me feel at home and truly had a heart of God's love. I made a lot of friends there and realized there was more to the Baptist denomination than good food at church picnics. They were truly dedicated to winning souls and teaching the word of God. I am thankful for my years spent there.

I was planning my oldest daughter's first birthday party when I had a dream that I was four months pregnant. Whenever I have a dream, I feel could be from God it is very vivid in color such as this one was. I was nursing and taking precautions and should not be able to conceive. I shared this with my sister, and she said she felt I was and should buy a test. I did and wound up at the doctor who told me I was about four months pregnant just like my dream. In August, I had another beautiful baby girl. Alexandria came into this world a lot quicker than Demetria. The doctor thought she would be a nine-pound baby and wanted to induce my labor. She came into this world a six pound baby at noon time after four hours of labor.

My husband decided to get involved in our little community after a kid was attacked by a pack of dogs. He soon became the volunteer marshal, or glorified dog catcher. He was authorized by the county Sheriff to hand out citations to residents that did not adhere to dog regulations. So, my husband became a target as did I. One night, Craig came home from doing his duties and had blood all over his shirt and face. I was pregnant with my oldest Demetria. Scared to death I cried, and he said, "Take me to the emergency room." It was a good forty-five minutes away. The police said we could not file charges, but he had been beat up by two men after giving them a citation about their dog. As time moved on; things got scary. Soon we were too scared to walk in the neighborhood as these men and their families grew to hate us. One day I noticed a hanging noose in the window of their home. It was said it was put there for us. One day driving by the house it was the only way in or out and the man pulled out a gun and waved it in the air making sure I saw it.

After the birth of Demetria, things calmed down a bit in the community. We continued once again to attend the community fair and try to be a good part of the little village. After about nine months of Demetria being born I was sitting out in our front yard of our freshly painted yellow house. The breeze was so nice, and fall was in the air. I was planning how I would decorate our little house and so happy my mom was finding joy and Craig seemed happy too. Life was pretty good then a *zip buzz splat*! Again! A bullet had buzzed by head and hit the tree where Demetria's swing hung from. I grabbed her and quickly ran inside screaming for mom. I called 911 and in five minutes at least six cop cars were in my front yard. After that, I begged Craig to move us out of there. I was so scared. But he was not too worried; he felt it would be ok.

But a few nights later, someone stopped in front of our home and left a paper bag on the porch and sat in their car running idle for a bit. When they drove away Craig checked, and it was human feces in the bag. I said I cannot raise my baby this way. He agreed if I could sell the house without advertising, he would move. He told me there was no way I could make it happen. Within two months we had a buyer and I found us a house in Crane, Missouri about twenty-five miles away. I was so happy!

CHAPTER 8

Matthew 22:37

After some time went by, my husband became unhappy again. We moved to a Presbyterian church, then Methodist then some off the wall cultist church and soon none at all. It got to the point where he refused to let me pray with my children or tell them about Jesus and to share what Easter or Christmas meant in the Christian faith. I had to pray with them in private or if he heard me, he would grow angry.

I was offered a position to be a worship leader and we headed out to church on a Sunday morning. Craig was driving, we began to fuss, and I was pregnant with Alexandria; my nerves were on edge. He kept going on how he wanted to stop the whole church thing and how I was raised in a cult and he wouldn't let his girls grow up in such an environment. I cried more and he said I needed to get a grip and try his way. I told him to turn around and take me home as my heart pounded out of my chest.

He soon put his foot down and told me to try it his way. He made me put all my gospel music and Bibles in a box that he placed in the attic. I grew angry at God. My heart began to harden, and I even tried learning about other spiritual avenues since he refused to let me have my relationship with Christ the way I wanted. I have always been a spiritual person and once you experience true spirituality in God, nothing else satisfies. Even for a season I was curious about other spiritual things, I could never deny the power of God. I was just feeling lost.

Soon politics is what filled his emptiness and we became involved in the Democratic party. I began to take interest as I was trying to save my marriage and keep our life somewhat happy for our children. We wrote and performed music for many Democratic events and became quite popular in Southwest Missouri. Soon I was President of the Democratic Club, chair of a bond issue committee for our local schools, president of the local park board, vice president of the PTA, and delegate for the Democratic convention. Getting so involved it led to me running for State Representative of the 141st District.

The *Nation* magazine sent a reporter from New York to write about me. She spent the whole day with me. The interview turned out pretty good, I thought. My name then was Deanna Hodges. I worked hard for the campaign and had many radio ads running on local Springfield and Branson, Missouri channels. I campaigned alongside Claire MacAskill, Governor Holden, and so many more. I had a great experience and am glad I experienced such a time in my journey. I did not win my district, but it was an amazing experience.

Cameron, my nephew was a sweet person. He loved old people and little kids. He had just turned twenty-two and landed a great modeling job locally. One night he was headed to get his and his girlfriend Lindsey their passports to go on a mission trip soon. As he was driving, a little old lady who was not supposed to be driving, was coming head on towards him and crossed the centerline. It took Cameron's life and injured Lindsey breaking her femur and glass cuts on her face and much more.

That night was so horrible for my sister and brother-in-law that I will not tell all in this book. But I will share some heavenly things with you. At Cameron's funeral, there were so many people the church couldn't hold them all. While we sat in the sermon some of us saw a white feather fall from the ceiling of the church. My sister looked to see later if she could find it and it was nowhere. Then as we set under the tent at the graveside the cold Missouri wind chilled my bones. As the preacher spoke, I couldn't help but cry and I and others saw a lone white feather drift down into the plants at the coffin side. Afterwards we looked and no sign of it.

A few days later, I was sitting out on our deck that was elevated above our backyard as the yard sloped down to a narrow road that was rarely traveled. I heard something fall through the trees. We lived in a pretty country area and very small town of Crane, Missouri. I squatted down behind the rails on my deck to see if I could see anything. I soon heard someone singing, it was a man. He was singing *I'll Fly Away*. As he got even with our back yard, I noticed he looked to be over six feet tall, maybe seven feet. The neighbor's dogs began to bark, and he calmly said, "Hey, what's your problem?" They laid down at his feet and hushed. He proceeded to pet them and stood up while looking up right at me. He put his coat over his shoulder and began singing, "*I'll Fly Away oh Glory, I'll fly away.*" He walked into the streetlight then disappeared. I have never seen him again, nor ever before.

One night, I was telling my girls stories at bedtime. They loved for me to lay between them and make up stories to tell them. I had just laid down with the lamp on and warm quilts covering us that my mother and grandmother had made us. As I started to read, my daughter said "Mom, look." I looked up and falling from the ceiling right onto me was a white feather. As it landed, we watched it hit the quilt and it just disappeared. We all three were looking at each other in dismay. It took us a bit then decided it must have been Cameron giving us a sign. After that, for several years, I would see a feather fall in my car or in my house knowing that it must have been a sign from heaven, and I had peace.

My oldest daughter started having nightmares at a young age. I started praying over her and one morning she came into the kitchen and said, "Mom, Jesus was in my room last night." I replied, "Oh, he was?" She said, "Yes, he told me no more bad dreams everything was going to be just fine." She stopped having nightmares.

When she started learning to talk, Demetria, my oldest, would tell me when she saw angels. She would just ask me if I saw them while showing me where they were and what color their clothes were. One day she told me about heaven. She said it was beautiful there. There are rivers, mountains, and trees. There are also birds and butterflies with colors like we have never seen here on the earth. I loved to hear her talk of heaven.

My youngest child, Alexandria, also spoke of heaven. I would listen closely. Remember, I was not allowed to take them to church so most of what they said had to come from God. We were riding in the van one day, my mom in the seat beside me, as I drove and the girls behind us in their car seats. Alexandria proceeded to speak up one day while going down the road. She said, "I didn't ask to come down here." I asked where she was talking about. She said, "You know, down here on Earth. I didn't ask to come down here." Because of all the things my girls said about heaven and God I became stronger in my faith.

Demetria has always been our artist, saxophone player, and humanitarian. Alexandria is our singer, cook, and science geek. What a blessing my girls have been to me. I would hate to think of going through all that I have without them. My daughters are probably what saved me. They showed me that God, heaven, Angels, and Jesus are truly real. Just because of how they spoke without being told of them and all the details.

CHAPTER 9

I Corinthians 13:4_8

My husband became unhappy with me. He started telling me he didn't love me anymore. He became very difficult to live with. We had a four-bedroom house, a pontoon boat, lake house, a successful business. It all looked so good. We were the family who had the most decorated house for Christmas. He played Santa at school for the kids. We were involved in every parade. We were the perfect family in the eyes of most. There were so many underlying problems no one knew.

I became so nervous my doctor put me on two different anxiety medicines and I started developing stomach problems. My chest would hurt when he got angry with me, and I was scared many times I was having a heart attack. I spent a couple of times in the emergency room just to find out it was stress.

I knew I had gained weight from all the stress of life and dealing with so much change. I tried everything to lose weight and I only failed over and over. My doctor said I had gained and couldn't lose due to the stress of my marriage. My husband became more unhappy with me. He accused me of getting fat to spite him. He used food and my children against me, and I only grew more hurt and angrier. I begged him to walk with me and exercise. He refused and said I was the one who needed to lose, not him, and he was ashamed of me. The hurt a woman feels when her husband speaks down to her is more painful than most people realize. I struggled everyday just to breathe. Somedays, I wished I could just stop breathing. If not for my girls I would have given up. I soon caught myself standing in the kitchen at 10 a.m. with a large glass of wine. I started crying and asked God to help me. I was so desperate for God to help.

I had to work by myself most days to help keep the business going as he laid in bed with depression. I tried everything I knew, I even called our family doctor and begged him to help. Of course, he couldn't do anything if I couldn't get my husband to his office. One dark afternoon I came home to my mom crying and Craig had rented a trailer and was loading my stuff inside it. No one else's stuff, just mine! I begged him to stop and asked how I could fix this. He asked me to go to Oklahoma, just leave. I called his doctor and they said they could do nothing unless he came in and he refused. He was already on anxiety medicine and I thought it might be causing issues for him. But that seemed to fade, and I stayed hoping God would work things out. Many times he offered to build me a bedroom in our basement and we would stay together until my girls graduated. We went almost another year after that before my world fell apart.

My mom did great at helping me with house chores and my girls. She has been my rock in so many ways. I tried to hide the truth from her of my marriage and I tried to act like everything was good. But she knew it was just a matter of time before something broke. So, she did her best to keep my girls busy while we fought and helped hide my crying from my girls many times.

The day came when my husband had enough and asked me to leave. He said he had stopped loving me years ago and how we should never have married. It wasn't the first time I heard this he had said several times the last four or five years. I was refusing to believe it, but I knew he wasn't happy. Three days earlier, I had prayed God would change him or give me a way out. I didn't believe this was happening to us. This happened right before bedtime and I was left sitting up alone on the couch crying and praying all night. I only got about three hours sleep that night and at six the next morning he woke up and asked me what I was going to do. He asked if I would stay to show him how to run our business then I could leave. I said, "No, if you want me to leave, today is a good day for me to leave." He took his usual cup of coffee and walked out the door.

I went to my mother's room crying and my babies were sleeping. I asked what she thought I should do. She said she didn't know the answer but supported me in my decision. I simply felt numb. How could someone just stop loving you like this? I was so shaky and weak from crying but, I felt I needed to leave and thought that maybe a few days away would be good for us.

I woke my girls that day we packed, and my mom drove to my sisters. Thinking I would be back. My heart was so broken. I was hopeful to go back home. I just knew he would change his mind and beg me to come back.

I cried all the way to Oklahoma. He refused to talk and told me to leave. I took my two girls to our lake house. I thought he would come for me or call asking what we could do to fix things. It never happened, what did happen was I received a phone call from his so-called pastor of a cult gathering church. He said I would never find a man to love me and that having children would greatly harm me in finding a future. He said it was best if I left my husband alone. That is what my husband wanted and asked him to tell me.

I waited, but the third night passed as I tried to comfort my girls and myself in our lake home with so many memories. That fourth morning I woke to an email in our business account. It was from a woman thanking my husband for a wonderful night. My heart sank as I read her email meant for him. Then I heard of others, she wasn't the only one. I tried to talk to him by phone, but he insisted he was done with me. He told me to go find my happiness because he found his. So, I filed for divorce. I had never been on my own. I had married him at the age of twenty leaving my dad's home, and I was truly scared.

Soon my husband asked me to leave the lake house because he had sold it and I couldn't stay any longer. I began to search what to do. Praying and asking family for advice. Hard times were surely ahead of my girls and me. But God's grace was sufficient.

My husband was sending child support and said he would help me in this change as much as he could. He even wanted to stay friends but that quickly changed.

A lady I had met let me rent a house from her and it was a great blessing. She also offered that I could use a store front she owned, as it was empty. I decided to try running a secondhand store.

One morning I was crying, and my youngest daughter Alexandria came to me and pretended to wrap a rope around me. She then pretended to pull it up tight. She said, "Now momma, you are not falling apart anymore." My girls and God gave me strength to keep going. Knowing we had lost everything except each other was very overwhelming. But I knew God would see us through somehow.

During this time, my girls were enrolled and attending school. I was trying to give them stability and a home as much as possible. At that time, my ex-husband was helping with child support. He started to fight me with taking that away and things got harder. I needed to buy food and when I went to use my account my card was declined because he went and closed my bank account. Many times, I hunted for coins to buy a kid's meal at a hamburger place and my girls and I would split the food in that meal. When I called my ex-husband to ask why he had done this, he said I had done this to myself. I spent many nights falling asleep crying and begging God to give me strength and wisdom.

For my store inventory I went to auctions, flea markets, and garage sales to get things cheap for my shop and even some people donated that were familiar with my story.

I had met back up with a guy who was the first guy I dated, and I fell into a wrong situation. I wound up falling for sweet words and married him. I was so lost and confused I couldn't think straight. He was not for me at all. Soon I filed for an annulment and was so relieved to clean up my mistake.

Meanwhile, I was invited to a revival service and being desperate to hear from God, I went. The evangelist took the stage and began singing a worship song. I cannot remember what it was. I do remember the rest. He stopped singing and his eyes fixed on me. I thought, *Oh my, he is going to point me out. No,no,no I don't want people to look at me.* But he said, "Young lady you are not here by accident, come forward." So, I did, and he took my hands and said, "Your life is being unraveled like a ball of tangled yarn. God is pulling it apart and he will put it back together and give you back everything you have lost." I thanked the Lord and had a good time of prayer. But when I left everything was still the same. I knew I had to start seeking God more. I recommitted my heart to him as I had grown cold the last few years.

It was Thanksgiving time. I was still struggling, one evening I sat down in the middle of the kitchen floor to cry. Praying God please help me. My cell phone rang. I wiped my tears and said "Hello?" A little lady's voice said, "Hello? Is this my granddaughter?" I said, "I don't think so unless you are calling from heaven. Both my grandmothers are passed on to heaven." The little lady said, "Oh I am sorry." Then she said, "Are you okay?" I began to weep. "Oh no, I am not okay." I spilled out what I was going through, and she prayed with me and offered encouraging words. She said hold on to God he will bring you through this. She said I am going to tell my niece about you.

Well, soon a knock at my door and I answered and saw this beautiful smile. She said you don't know me, but my Aunt Barbara talked to you on the phone the other night. I am Debbie and I have brought some food and some clothing for your daughters. I again had to weep. She said our church is giving away Thanksgiving meals, come by and get one for you and the girls. We did and we made new friends. Thank you, God, for never forgetting us!

CHAPTER 10

Joshua 1:9

Soon things began to change, my friend needed the building I was using as a store and so I talked with my girls and we decided to head to Texas. I lived there in the 1980's to 1992, so I had friends there. Trying to keep things as normal as possible, I would make it fun with girls and told them each time we had to make a change we were going to try a different piece of cake. We had chocolate now we will try vanilla. Texas here we come!

But things were harder than I expected. Living out of my Jeep and staying some with a friend and my family I found an extended stay place to rent by the week. I enrolled my girls in Texas schools and began to look for a job.

Meanwhile, my ex-husband remarried, and I thought he was moving on with his new life.

I felt so alone and scared many times. My daughters brought me joy and encouragement. We became even closer and I am so thankful for the time we spent together. I made it as enjoyable as I could. Swimming every chance we got, and trying out new stores to venture into even though buying things were not an option, we had fun anyway. I apologized many times to my girls for not being able to buy things for them and always they replied with, "It's okay, mom. We don't need stuff we are okay." They sacrificed plenty. My youngest girl wore broken glasses put together with tape to school. My oldest wore worn out shoes that hurt her feet. I still cry thinking of their love for me not to complain but held on strong and helped me to overcome.

One day, my girls and I went to the thrift store and found a pot and some cooking utensils. That night we were making some soup and a knock happened at the door of the extended stay place we were at. I slowly opened the door, and it was a Texas Ranger. He was very rude and insisted I was a criminal. He spoke angrily to me and said I had run away with my kids and didn't tell anyone. He had brought papers to serve me that my ex was trying to take my daughters away.

This was far from the truth. I told my family where I was and put my girls in school and was making the best I could, and we were making progress as I had a job interview that week.

I would take my girls to meet up with my ex-husband or to his parents at least every two weeks or so. I never wanted them to lose their relationship with their dad. So, one weekend I drove them up to their grandparents in Oklahoma and dropped them off on a Friday afternoon. On the next day, which was Saturday, I was visiting Kirk and he had to go to his apartment office. I received a phone call from my ex-husband and he asked, "Are you sitting down?" I said, "No." "Then you need to Deanna," he said. He told me how he had gone to his parents and got there at midnight. He woke the girls and made them get in his truck with the help of his new wife and took them to our old home in Missouri.

My heart sank, as my girls were everything to me and he was only trying to use them to hurt me. He told me I would never see them again and how they would not be allowed to talk to me. I sank to the floor as my heart broke in pieces and after he hung up, I sobbed, and Kirk walked in. He grabbed me and asked if I was okay and what had happened. When I explained he said, "Call your lawyer now." I did and my lawyer said they are supposed to be in my custody and if I could get them back in a public place, I could bring them home. So, days went by and I tried to get the police, the sheriff, anyone who had been our friends to go check on them. The police said there was absolutely nothing they could do. My girls finally got a message through to me how scared they were. How they wanted to come back to me and feared my ex because of his behavior and he would not let them outside the house. I cried so much and asked God to help the fear in me and protect my babies.

Kirk had me call the police, the sheriff, and my lawyer again. They said if you see them in the street or away from the old house of ours, I could get them and go back across the state line and he could not do anything to get them back. So, we made a plan with my oldest girl through messenger online. They were to meet us at 2 a.m. in the back street of our old home. Kirk and I drove all day to get there. We pulled into the street at 1:55 a.m. and I messaged Demetria, no answer. I had told her to set an alarm to be awake when we were coming. Finally, a reply, *Coming now!* We waited in the street with thick fog all around and could hardly see five feet in front of the car. We waited, and finally coming through the fog was Demetria carrying her saxophone and Alexandria carrying her stuffed cat and suitcase. They were crying because it was a steep hill and they had slipped a few times getting down to us. We got them in the car and drove off as fast as we could headed for the state line. I was so relieved to get them back. We all cried from joy and relief.

When we were back together, and I kept them even closer knowing that it could happen again. I went to court to limit his visits as he proved I could not trust him. That was a relief to know we were safe.

I was in the office paying my weekly rent, when a woman overheard me talking to the clerk. She brought me her business card and said, "God has laid it on my heart to treat you and your daughters to dinner." I accepted her offer and we met her for dinner that night. She explained she was in real estate and was a Christian. She said God shows her people to help and He had laid me on her heart. I told her I was looking for a job and she told me of a lady who had a cleaning business and needed help. I called the lady and spent the next month working for her and took on extra work to have a down payment to rent a cute little home in Dallas.

She paid me before I even did the job, and I went to rent the house for my girls and me. It was Christmas, and she sent her husband to leave a box of groceries on my porch. I have yet to reconnect with these two precious ladies. Maybe they were angels sent to help us.

Finally, a home once again!

I didn't realize at the time how much trauma I had gone through. I was so focused on surviving and keeping my babies safe. Many sleepless nights and days with worry of being able to buy groceries. Opening the refrigerator and seeing nothing but empty shelves and the cabinets too were bare. I applied for food stamps and was able to get food for my girls. We were so excited to go grocery shopping! Cereal, milk, chicken, soup, and even a bit of ice cream! Every time one of us opened a door you would hear thank you Jesus! We have food!

My daughters really took to the school in Dallas their grades soared. I was so happy at how well they were doing. I asked them every week if they were happy. Always, the answer was, "Yes mom, we are happy." My oldest even said, "I finally found where I fit in." So, we stayed, and the vanilla cake was tasting pretty good.

My oldest took the saxophone like her father and soared in her talent along with art. She won awards, I have lost track of how many. I took her to enroll in high school and she tried out for a high school band. I was standing in the room with other parents and kids who were waiting to try out for the high school band. This school was known as being the best in marching band music. Well, she started warming up that sax. Everyone got quiet. The band teacher came rushing out of his practice room and said, "Who was that?" I looked around, everyone was still, and I pointed to my daughter. He said, "Girl, you are in!" She did well in band until a new teacher came in and was very harsh on everyone. Kids lost their desire to perform.

Meanwhile, she was also in an art cluster. You see, my girls were accepted into magnet schools. That is quite an honor. So, art and music were Demetria's clusters. The art teacher said she was about two to three years above the other students. He said she would really succeed if she sticks with it. She earned scholarships and awards to go to Southern Methodist University here in Dallas. She has her own art business as Dannidoodles.com. Doing commissions, books, advertisements, humanitarian projects, and caricatures at events.

Alexandria soared in choir and band playing her clarinet. She also earned many awards. One day her counselor called and said, "I want you to know your daughter is very smart. Not just smart, Einstein smart." She said, "This girl will do well." She went on to Southern Methodist University as well with scholarships and awards. She has just applied to nursing school and is working as a youth leader in our church as well as worship leading on the worship team at our church.

One night around 3 a.m., there was loud knocking on our door. Scared, I went to the door and asked who it was. It was the police. They said my life might be in danger and I needed to be aware that my ex-husband was headed our way according to his wife. I was very afraid as I thought he was happy and settled in with his new wife. Although, they had recently sold our old home and moved to Texas too. His wife and parents did find him after a day or so and he had gone south instead of north to us. He was put in care of his parents and has undergone therapy to hopefully restore him to health. I never wished anything bad on him. I just wanted to be free to live life. He had asked me to leave and told me he didn't love me anymore but it seemed he didn't want me to move on. I know now he had many issues mentally he was dealing with that I didn't understand when we were together. I do think that was a big part of our failed marriage and I forgive him and put it all in God's hands.

Backing up just a bit. I have known Kirk since I was a young child. We attended some of the same churches together with our families. Kirk and I dated as teenagers, and since I was older I picked him up in my Scout. I had a crush on him most of my life and worked to catch his attention from all the other girls at church. But, finally after thirty years, here we were.

Kirk played country music every weekend with a band or two doing what he loved to do. I would go every chance I could just to support him. I witnessed to women about the Lord as we would sit and listen to the band. The winter was cold but no snow. Kirk and I sat in my car on his break. It was almost February 29th; a leap year. If you are familiar with the tradition, the girl can propose to the guy only at leap year. My grandmother Laningham at the age ninety-six, had given me permission to ask him to marry me. So, I did! I ordered a fortune cookie and after we ate a buffet of Chinese food I gave it to him. He said "Yes" by the way!

My nightmares started again. I would wake up screaming like I was being tortured. I had to try to find peace. So, we started looking for a church and I started looking for a counselor.

During this time, we started attending Lake Pointe Church in Rockwall, Texas. In the same building I had visited when it was a very charismatic church back in the 80's! The first time I attended, Pastor Steve Stroop was the senior Pastor. He hit my heart head on. I was so touched by God and I knew that was the church for me. Every time we went God spoke! No matter what we dealt with that following week whether it be an argument, financial problems, family, stress, we could count on God to use Pastor Steve to preach to us! I am so happy we found this church and we now have an amazing new senior Pastor Josh Howerton! Wow! God still is speaking to us! It is a Baptist church, by the way, and man, can you feel God!

Kirk was used to the nightlife and he played every weekend in a club or dance hall. I was searching and never felt completely like I belonged. My heart was hungry for God. I started spending more time in prayer and my hunger for God just got stronger. I began to pray more, and I told God, "I want my calling Lord. I want my gifts. I give my heart and soul completely to you."

During this time, I found a wonderful counselor, Apree Clicque. She has been a God send to me. All the time growing up, I heard you should never go to a counselor or psychiatrist because God would heal you on His own. But I learned that God uses counselors too! I went to her about my nightmares. I sat on her couch as my hands were sweaty and my heart pounded. I couldn't hardly talk about what had happened to me. My tears began to flow when I explained how I had gotten to where I was. She spoke so kindly and gave me instructions how to start to heal. My homework was to sit down and write myself a letter. As I wrote down my letter which was to tell myself I was worth something and that I have value even though I felt had been thrown away. I remember how I wept writing the words, Dear Deanna, you are not trash! You are special and someone will love you the way you deserve. *You are going to be okay. I felt such heaviness in my chest, and I cannot explain the feeling of, Why? Why did he tire of me? Why did I get thrown away? Why was I not good enough?* Learning to understand I am good enough. I am worth something has been a ten-year journey. I still struggle somedays with panic that my husband will grow tired of me and it will all end.

Recently the counselor said, "Put down the suitcase. No one is going anywhere." Do you know how that feels to come to that? I realized after a few days of hearing that, I am home, I am loved, it isn't going to be over; he isn't throwing me away too! I still weep as I think of those words. My heart yearns to be truly loved and I was so scared I would be thrown away again and I have lived on edge since 2010 that I would never find home again. But I have! I am home, I am loved!

That's when I truly started feeling whole. I still have a strong desire to work for God. The music business can swallow you up and can make it hard to stay focused on God. But I know God is faithful and even though I am not in ministry at this moment I pray daily that the right door will open. I am a firm believer in prayer and fasting. If you seek God, you WILL find Him. God has healed a lot of my heart. I have come to understand that I forgive my ex and realize he was struggling with mental health issues I was not aware of. I pray for him and I hope if you are reading this book and going through a similar situation, I am praying for you as well. I know God will meet you where you are. Never give up!

On June 1, 2012 Kirk and I married. It was a sweet day, and I will never forget it. We went to the Justice of Peace and Demetria and Alexandria witnessed. It was a new start to a new adventure.

Guest on The Penny Gilley Show this Friday is **Deanna G. Priddy**, 2:30 pm on RFD-TV with a repeat on Saturday morning at 6:00 am...

My husband Kirk and I started our band *Unbroken*. We felt that the name represented our lives and wanted to use it as a testimony to others. Hoping others would see that life can be good and no matter what you have gone through you can remain UNBROKEN. We play music that is clean and family friendly. It has given us the opportunity to meet a lot of people and even witness to so many. We have had the honor of opening for Mickey Gilley, Johnny Rodriquez, John Connelly, and others in the music business.

Chapter 10

In 2018, I saw that *The Voice* was coming to Dallas and I mentioned signing up. My family highly encouraged me to do so. On the day of auditions, I woke up and decided I wouldn't go. You know all the excuses: I am too old now, it's a waste of time, I am not that good anyway. My youngest daughter pleaded with me to go as she knew I always had a dream of singing. So, I got ready and made plans to meet my friend Sheila as she was my support that day. I pulled into the parking lot and it was so crowded I began to get afraid and wanted to back out. I went on in as the hot Texas sun hit my face and a bead of sweat rolled down my brow, I said, *Daddy, this is for you today*. I got my ID bracelet and found a seat amongst hundreds of other singers. Joyful singing began and before long we were all singing together *Lean on Me*! Several of us were rounded up and taken to a waiting area where we were then called into a room. We were told to sit in a circle and asked individually to sing a part of our song we had chosen. After eliminations I was the only female left among three guys. It wasn't long and I was the only one left. I had made it! I was chosen! When I walked out of that stadium with my red ticket applause broke out and I cried. Thankfully, I went after all and was so excited. I had two more auditions to go through before the big one in front of the judges in California! I made it through to the last one and my song choice was not right, and I was asked to retry next time.

Genealogy has been a hobby of mine for many years. My dad always said our family had nothing to be proud of and felt like he was a nobody. But after he passed in 1995 at the young age of fifty-eight, I started digging even more into our family tree. Then my sister Belinda jumped on board and we have learned so many amazing things!

When I was young, I remember my great aunt my grandmother Wood's sister was always going to Israel. She had stacks of papers everywhere in her living room. It was her genealogy research! Well, we found out why she visited Israel. We found out on my Dad's side we are descended from the Tribe of Judah! This might explain the miracles that followed him. Also, the House of Stuart and King James who interpreted the Bible is my eleventh great grandfather! With knights Templars as grandfathers and direct lines of kings my dad would be surprised! Not to mention Chief Pushmataha, my grandfather, and many Native warriors as uncles, cousins, and grandfathers. All DNA proven. I am also proud to represent the Cheraw Native Tribe in Texas.

Then on my mother's side, I am descended from the Tribe of Levites! One of my favorites is Abraham the Patriarch is my 100th Grandfather! We never knew this, nor did any of our family. We also have the House of Stuart on this side and Knights Templars, as well as Pocahontas, a great grandmother, and many other Native Americans also of the old Choctaw the Tribe of Cheraw.

I am so thankful God has shown my heritage to me. I am proud to pass it on to my daughters.

After about five years married, we lost my mother-in-law Rachel to Hodgkins Lymphoma. We thought she had won the battle, but it came back and hit hard. We were with her when she passed. Just like when dad left this world; I felt her spirit leave too. She was one of my most favorite people. I loved my time with her as we often talked about God and how He was so good. She had seen many revivals too and answered prayers. I truly miss her beautiful smile and sweet spirit. She never met a stranger and offered her kindness to everyone.

One of my saddest days was when my grandmother Laningham left this world. She was my mom's mother and was such an angel. She taught me how to treat people kindly and how a Godly woman is to live. She loved her family dearly and I never heard her say an ugly or angry word to or about anyone. She had been widowed in her late forties and never married again. She said grandpa was all the man she ever needed. She was raised Baptist but was filled with the Holy

Ghost in one of my dad's church services so they teased her that she was a "Bapticost." I spent many hours with her every chance I got. I loved staying all night with her and watching old cowboy shows while eating her buttermilk pancakes.

Granny had been the rock of our family. She taught us about entertaining angels, unaware how to be kind in case someone was an angel sent to test us. She was a strong yet very gentle woman. Growing up in the Oklahoma hills around Brock, Oklahoma. She was a woman who could get things done. She once dug a well so her family could have water, she built their chicken shed, repaired a lot of things that broke and never complained a bit. One time she became terribly ill and since she lived alone, no one was there to help her. She said she was cold, and an angel came in and pulled the covers up over as she laid there on the bed. I still can smell those white cotton sheets as she hung them on the clothesline singing in the sweet by and by.

We were often going to Oklahoma to visit my father-in-law, as he lived alone since Rachel passed. We helped him around the house as much as he needed. One afternoon he said he had gotten in contact with an old sweetheart from his youth. She had not forgotten him and said she was always in love with him. Well, he went to Washington state to see her with Kirk's sister Karen and was love struck. He actually asked her to marry and wanted to bring her back to Oklahoma. Her name is Oleta. She was the wife of a minister who had passed many years before. So, two lonely sweethearts got married! They married for only three months when we lost Kirk's dad Kenneth to pneumonia and internal bleeding. Our hearts were broken once again.

Proud of the family God has given me, and my close family now consists of my husband Kirk, my sweet daughters Demetria and Alexandria. My mother lives in Missouri still and is an amazing woman of faith. She still reads her Bible every morning and night without fail. I can always call on her for prayer and God seems to hear her.

I inherited a sweet step-daughter Lauren and her beautiful daughters Kaydence, Trinity, Destiny and Kimber. Also, two step-sons Ryan and Tyler and their children Jayden, Arianna, and Niyjah. Kirk has two sisters Retha and Karen, one brother Rick and their children Brandon, Kenny, Alecia, Ray, Russell, Isaac, and Leah.

My oldest sister Sheila and my brother-in-law Lavoy their three children Gwyn, Alicia, and Seth who have their own children. Sheila is a loving person who shares God's love with everyone who crosses her path and still paints. Her faith and wisdom still helps hold me together.

My next sister Theresa and brother-in-law Billy; their children Jamie, Frankie, Kase, Stacey, Bo, and Denna who have their own children and grandchildren. Theresa went through the army and made Sargent, she was also an amazing body builder and succeeded at so much. She has been an example of strength to me.

Next to me in age, is my sister Belinda and brother-in-law Rusty, their son in heaven Cameron and their son Nathan, his sons and one daughter. Belinda is a minister and an author, and I hope to share writing with her someday. She recently purchased a Hammond organ for their church. I believe a revival is about to break out in Branson, Missouri! Belinda has been a spiritual leader for me, and I lean often on her wisdom of spiritual things. She is a warrior for God. She and Rusty are worldwide missionaries.

I am thankful for what God is doing in their lives. Praising God that they know who Jesus is hopefully by the life we live, and that he is with them in this journey called life.

I am sitting now in the living room of our beautiful home God has blessed us with. My girls are doing great. My husband has a successful business and mine is doing well too. My heart desires more of God and I am trying to keep an open ear and heart to His will. God has worked many miracles in and around me. He has taken all that I have been through and made me a stronger and happier woman. My nightmares have greatly decreased, I am happier and look forward to the new day every morning now.

Unfortunately, in March, coronavirus hit here in Texas and for six months we have not been able to perform with our band, nor function in our normal routines. I have not seen my mother in over eight months and likewise with my husband's family. Although, we are enjoying time at home, I believe I have time to finish my story for you. I have grown another year older and am now fifty-four years old. I can say everything I lost has been replaced just like the prophecy the minister told me how my life was being unraveled but, God would put it back together He would restore everything I lost and I would be made whole. I do not know how anyone makes it without God to lean on. God has restored us and is still working on our lives. Don't give up if you are struggling and going through heartbreak. God will be there for you!

Things are not always perfect, but God's grace is, and if you hold on joy comes in the morning! If your life is in a tangled mess such as mine was, God can also unravel your life and make you whole again as He did for me!

Please feel free to contact Deanna to share your testimony or to book Deanna for speaking or the band *Unbroken*!

www.facebook.com/unraveled

email: unraveledandmadewholeagain@aol.com

www.thebandunbroken.com

If you would like to contact my sister Belinda for bookings here is her page. www.facebook.com/booksbybelinda

For caricatures check out my daughters art www.dannidoodles.com